Small Verses

"so I stand here testifying to small and great"
Acts 26:22

Haiku

Written by Karen Rhodes-Ochoa

To all my girls: Katy, Sydney, Jessica, Vera, Lena, Tessa and Amanda. Ya'll have loved, inspired and supported me. I am beyond grateful for each one of you. Thank you for being my constant source of strength and light.

Not to be constrained by the greatest thing, but to be contained in the smallest thing, is divine.

C. 1640, Anonymous inscription in a volume commemorating the 100th anniversary of the founding of the Jesuits.

Table of Contents

Part 1

Wider Seasons of Meaning

Summer *Wings of Light Conversation*

1

Empty coffee cups.
Wings of light conversation
flutter above the table.

2

Painted roses, scone crumbs
littered across bone china plate.
Early morning leavings.

3

Teaspoons of sunshine—
life's fragile ingredients
measured in moments.

4

Soft June days arrive—
a sigh after May's howling
uprooting darkness.

5

The night sky swallows
all the bleeding full moon—
a single crimson gulp.

6

Summer's slow progress,
gently sanctifying warmth,
breathes upon each new day.

7

Proud mourning dove struts
convinced of his own comfort—
neighbor's cat pounces!

8

Quiet breeze rustles
cardinal's folded ruby
feathers—God's whisper.

9

Yellow rock daisies
bob a radiant curtsy
to afternoon's sun.

10

As days grow longer,
faith spreads beneath the oak tree—
life's purple shadows.

11

Incumbent grey clouds
grumble, at last crumble—
it begins to rain!

12

Dawn withdraws—reveals
hushed lake at mighty oak's feet,
remnants of night's storm.

13

Rare mid-summer rains,
plane delays—so, on the road
like Jack Kerouac.

14

July's soaking rain
refreshes hot, thirsty ground—
mesquite flowers bloom.

15

Stormy afternoon,
between peals of thunder
the ice-cream van's bell?

16

On high desert plains
familial confusion
soaks the sandy soil.

17

Falsehood becomes truth
when small, lying seeds emerge—
dishonesty blooms.

18

Five patriotic
crows march across my brown lawn—
salute rising sun.

19

Sharp squinting sunlight—
piercing silhouette sketches
God's embodiment.

20

Heat lightening rolls
across humid dark night sky—
summer's fisted threat.

21

Loss and summer's heat
burn away arrogant pride—
ashes, dust remain.

22

Painted ladybugs
run over my writing desk,
fleeing summer's heat.

23

Cicada molts, flees
his sculpted now-empty skin
clinging to the screen.

24

Not native Texan,
incardinated fox hunts
small and great alike.

25

Remodeled crevice
under a rocky outcrop
hides newborn red fox.

26

Skunk with her kit held
safe in her mouth—love impels—
the open church doors.

27

Summer storms rattle
cups, plates upon the altar.
Quiet! And, be still!

28

Family storms break
wedded branches, uprooted stirps,
kith scattered like leaves.

29

Doughnut hole of blue
reveals truth and beauty
in a cloudy world.

30

Dog day cicadas
in the watches of the night
sing, *Rejoice, rejoice!*

31

Desperate weather,
a night shower of sorrows
tosses dreams of remorse.

32

A small smudge appears
staining the mirror's round edges—
eclipse of my soul.

33

Sow seeds as you go—
the harvest will be gathered
next season, perhaps.

34

Leaden clouds gather
rankling souls day after day—
grey quarrels erupt.

35

Purple deer pea vetch
wind their tiny tendrils around
God's dear wounded heart.

36

Calm praying mantis,
angelic pose may fool—but
he eats laity.

37

Summer breeze beckons,
enjoy my gentle caress,
balm for your vexed soul.

38

Orange ladybug flies
through my truck's open window,
then flies off again.

39

Exultantly perched
upon Saint Francis's bald head,
the mockingbird laughs.

40

Mockingbird so laughs
at the furled foolish shadows,
perched upon his pole.

41

Darkness slowly creeps,
night's cold fog stilling my heart—
my soul's penumbra.

42

Noonday eclipse: light,
then dark—divided nation.
Awe, wonder unites.

43

As the earth prospers
and hallowed gardens flourish,
so will justice reign.

44

Midafternoon breeze,
relaxing conversations
under the oak tree.

45

Celadon evening—
porcelain rains softly glaze
billowing nimbus.

46

Summer barefoot joy—
cast off leathered, woolen thoughts.
Laugh and play, freed heart!

47

Foggy morning love,
new Heights over Pacific—
Thirty years together.

Fall *Lengthening Shade*

1

Summer's sweet blue notes
slide into fall's field hollers—
a harvest of loss.

2

Black ravens arrive,
hummingbirds fly away south—
summer glides into fall.

3

Morning dew lingers
in maple's lengthening shade
baptizing summer.

4

Daylilies spent—brown
stalks kneel before waning noon,
summer's splendor yields.

5

The garden rebirth
after summer's heated trial—
flowering praises.

6

September morning,
our labor is sanctified—
plentiful harvest.

7

Elms slowly undress
as September falls away—
dropping defenses.

8

Fall arrives early,
grey clouds, north winds, constant rain—
festival dampened.

9

Sun, sea, sun, the Pope—
salty renewal of faith,
autumn beach retreat.

10

Wave's surging voice prays,
Hallowed is all creation,
on earth, in heaven.

11

Purple and green kite
laughs in the cloudless blue sky
and the waves clap on . . .

12

Abandoned shade tent,
summer's fun memorial
swallowed by fall seas.

13

Solitary walk
along the deserted shore—
autumn's scrutiny.

14

Dense brewing rain clouds
grip the straight true horizon,
taunt warm beach sunlight.

15

Lavender glory
bursts forth with the rising sun,
spreading sandy joy.

16

My dear hummingbirds,
did you flee coming winter
while I vacationed?

17 (Birth of Teresa Rose)

Will you gather what
your two sisters sow—truth and light—
or harvest thornless roses?

18

Fall under the dirt—
wait for the seed coat to split,
patience emerges.

19

Wistful chickadee,
your shrill notes mimic black bird's—
why not sing your song?

20

Little chickadee
curious, friendly chatter
welcomes the stranger.

21

Alone, the lily
stalwart in a vast littered field—
God's eternal truth.

22

What is dying now
shall arise, as did Nain—
the promise of life.

23

Fields of goldenrod
wave good morning to fall days—
aaachoo, make me sneeze!

24

Steady autumn rain—
morning smells of heavy humus,
yet my soul is light.

25

Slippery elm pods
cradled by kind autumn winds,
gently borne aloft.

26

Sliced by red two-edged
frond displayed on the altar—
so my heart can see.

27

Unholy thoughts, words
spread like dry-grass fire, burning
trust and character.

28

Peopling the path
beside two tiny rock hewn tombs,
the family prays.

29

Beautiful feet
sent to walk untrodden paths—
a relevant hike.

30

Gabriel's forest—
an announcement perched above
winding serpent creek.

31

Roots firmly planted,
prayerful branches raise their hands
toward bountiful light.

32

Darkness suddenly
exclaimed to the rising moon,
Where did daylight go?

33

Fall leaves scuttle
relentlessly down the road—
O, time forges on.

34

Consider the crows,
not the flashy cardinals—
God loves ugly birds.

35

Monarchs say, *Look at me,*
open their wings, flash of colors—
pay attention to joy!

36

Yarn over, knit one
pattern suddenly switches—
slip a stitch, bind off.

37

Cold strolled in last night,
without a preamble
not intent on staying awhile.

38 (Birth of Veronica Louise)

New life born in truth,
beauty, goodness and joy—
visiting Vera.

39

No sweeter duty
to praise God—love a child,
behold human life.

40

Living verdant faith
grows deep roots—sturdy vines wrap
abounding trellis.

41

Cloudless autumn sky
blue wideness redounds mercy,
echoes liberty.

42

Morning's golden heat
enfolds me in her fiery prayer,
fiercely rocks my soul.

43

Cardinal family
splash in the garden sprinkler—
recalling summer.

44

Born a daydreamer—
beauty, never out of reach
reaps silver linings.

45

Beauty sighs, beckons—
her glimmering coaxes us,
soft one-finger touch.

46

Majestic maple
wise, wrinkled, yet followed Him
tall into the light.

47

Yellow maple leaves,
butterflies waltz con moto
across fall's ballroom.

48

Advent is coming,
poor purple sorry season—
change my bleak heart, Lord.

Winter *Walking to a Cold Future*

1

White-tailed neighbors
have donned their grey winter coats
anticipating . . .

2

A star fell tonight—
writing heavenly haiku
on my way back home.

3

Pieces of the sky
fell into my lap today—
shivering pother!

4

Weak winter sunshine
doesn't warm my up-turned face,
but touches my soul.

5

Frosty wind carries
the scent of snowy cookies
across frozen yard.

6

Brown grass snaps, crunches,
walking to a cold future—
a love has ended.

7 (Birth of Magdalena Ann)

Early Christmas feast
interrupted by Lady
Magdala's advent.

8

Mirror of Holy,
my grandmotherly soul—
soft lap of safety.

9 (Rome)

Holy doors open,
pilgrims seeking forgiveness —
Mercy's Jubilee!

10 (Rome)

David, mouth twisted
releasing the mortal stone —
a slingshot grimace.

11 (Rome)

Warm flesh of marble
rendered alive — face, beard, hair —
by the sculptor's hand.

12 (Rome)

God's frail creation
projection of fragile light —
our common home.

13 (Rome)

Painter wields his brush
color, shadow, texture, strokes—
reveal His story.

14

Glory on the fields
yields the virgin's gilded *yes*—
fragrant holiness.

15

Silent holy night,
story whispered by a star,
guiding light of joy.

16

Christmas lights come down,
no joy proclaimed to the world—
Kings not yet arrived!

17

But my church is bright—
nativity's visitors
kneeling, offering gifts.

18

Atoning candle
emanates its gift of life—
pure immolation.

19

Pink sunset glow wraps
her arms around bare oak trees—
dusk comforts winter.

20

As if he knows she's
gone, cardinal confidently
pecks the fallen seed.

21

The howling wind tricks
me into believing I
hear her pleading cry.

22

Anxiously waiting,
her little glass bowl cradles
stale fish pellets.

23

Premium chicken
salad box still, yet cuddles
lonely red blanket.

24

Comfy curled cat,
a soft pillow of sorrow—
I miss your purring . . .

25

Red buds are not red,
but glorious amethyst—
winter's brightest jewels.

26

Raindrops and wren's cry,
early morning melody
expels winter's gloom.

27

Creation subject
to our sin, futility—
sadly miscarries.

28

Nine prayers of Jude
triumph of Christ's death, rising—
help our dire cause.

29

Showy coronas
atop crowds of stalks emerge
from winter's cold soil.

30

A quiet living
silence in the depth of breath —
inhale God's wisdom.

31

Trill Be Bop Whee Whee —
little wren on the kitchen sill
greets a cold new day.

32

The herds slowly munch
the dawning orb, bronze grasses
digest morning's light.

33

Like a light upon
a lampstand—high on a hill
shines big-box Walmart.

34

Clouds, like gold ribbons
sewn on the sky, stitch closed
the year's final day.

35

Winter loiters—loathed
to pick up her snowy skirts,
or stomp muddy boots.

36

My kitchen window
faces east, I lift my face,
eyes closed—feel the light.

37

Santa Anna wind
picks up her gossamer skirts
runs off, mists in tow.

38

Home again, my eyes
adjust to sage green winter
and wide Texas skies.

39

Cold constant raining
outside and inside my soul,
grey thoughts flood my heart.

40

A barren hollow
house, if not filled with kindness—
useless strife will clutter.

41

Foggy reflection
how you look misty at me—
frosty winter thoughts.

42

Winter wind shoved clouds
out of the sky—tumbled chairs
across frozen grass.

43

Silly Bradford pears,
blooming in still of winter—
pierced delicate buds.

44

Sunlit turquoise sky
holds no warmth in her bosom—
winds have ripped her bare.

45

Winter's long shadow
recedes, redeemed by the Lord
of light, salvation.

46

Twisted, ugly limbs
seen with eyes of love become
buds, flowers, new leaves.

47

Redbud blooms shiver
under a layer of ice—
spring's arrival stalled.

Spring *Vivid Red Dreams*

1

The nightjar arises
from winter's numbing slumber,
prays, *poor will, poor will.*

2

Missus Spring Wren chides
her husband's new nest attempt—
the often-used grill.

3

Spring teases and plays
hide and seek with the north wind—
frost and the warm sun.

4

Spring winds scatter our
winter ashes, discontent—
sweeping clean our hearts.

5

Take the bitter words
out of my mouth, rue blither
blather, swallow hard.

6

Spit cruel ashen words
out of my repentant heart—
anoint with hymns, Lord.

7

Twenty-one martyrs
dressed in orange, knelt in the sand—
beheaded for Christ.

8

Would I be willing
to prostrate in the grave surf—
die for the love of Christ?

9

Marked for Christ—ashes
smeared in a cross on foreheads—
witness to the world.

10

Ashes and sackcloth
wrap around dug up root ball—
buried sins exposed.

11

A single vinca,
Lenten purple bloom, confirmed
with dust and ashes.

12

Lenten thunderstorm
shatters, shakes, drenches, unloads—
slowly staggers on.

13

Truth cries out—seeking
salvation beneath her wings,
an eloquent nest.

14

A child's memory—
narrative of living yarn
which knits her to God.

15

We had such hope for
new beginnings, joyous growth—
hope is never dead.

16

Burning fallen branches,
spring cleaning so summer's fruit
an abundant yield.

17

Tender bare branches
swelling with possibility —
quiet sign of spring.

18

Water and blood flow
from deep new wounds in the tree —
bird pecks with fury.

19

Apple buds adorn
the altar of sacrifice.
Rejoice! And be glad!

20

Dawn's rosy hue sings:
Rejoice! By grace you are saved.
Come live in His light.

21

Consider lilies,
Easter trumpets singing praise—
lofty golden lisle.

22

Raspberry finch chants
outside my kitchen window—
Easter homily.

23

Blue blazing stars
tilt rayless heads heavenward—
bruised resurrection.

24

Diet of milkweed
gives the monarch bitter taste—
emboldened spirit.

25

Butterfly's beliefs
before wings—shaped by fat worm's
eat-and-grow commandments.

26

God cried all today
raining reconciling tears—
flooding forgiveness.

27

Overnight, world turned
bright—neon green, fluorescent
purple, light renewed!

28

Wild poppies sing,
*Alleluia! Spring rains have
ended Lenten drought.*

29

Low murmur wakes me—
far off thunder, my husband's voice
reading the Gospel.

30

Heron waits behind
his companion with a pole
for a fish dinner.

31

Sunflower dry bones
litter the bare dunes until buried
by shifting spring sands.

32

Sulphur butterfly
gazes into blue bonnet's
many sweet white eyes.

33

One grave rock daisy
stands sentry, guarding legions—
wayward blue bonnets.

34

Wild, ragged paint brush
dipped in vivid red dreams
illuminates my yard.

35

Longer evening sounds—
children's cheers, mowers muttering,
setting sun's laughter.

36

April storms beat upon
March wildflowers, pummeling
until submission.

37

Adumbral spring rain
falls continuous, cruel—
muddying clean souls.

38

Gladiola sprays,
reminder of funerals—
death, not birth, new life.

39

Hesitant dawn sun
regards the day, determines
not to show her face.

40

One more cloudy day
hallmark of this spring season—
dark, wet, damp and green.

41

Wind bending, looping
dancing through the metal struts—
bell tower whistlings.

42

Blooming everyday
wisdom comes with room to grow—
seed, bud, flower, death.

43

Worm-eaten laurel
seeks revenge with new green growth,
loving purple blooms.

44

Branches wrap His heart—
forsythia forgiveness,
merciful yellow buds.

45

Wilted peace lilies
litter the sanctuary —
sign of hardened hearts.

46

Spring storms, thunder shout
difficult days are over —
June's yellow joy comes!

47

Sirens greet the day —
rain, rain, Shoal Creek cascades —
Memorial Floods.

48

Dove descends, white light
poured into the world — our hearts'
indwelling spirit.

Part 2

Breathing Mystery

1

Barefoot we are born
because God knitted us precisely
to walk on holy ground.

2

Eve, defying God,
ate that fruit. Boom! transformed us—
shame, mistrust entered.

3

Seeds of blasphemy
planted deep in our heart's soil—
pluck those lying weeds!

4

Cold hurt seeps from pores,
permeates the sacristy—
freezes God's warm love.

5

Flame and thornless rose
embrace and dance, redeeming
our hurts, wounds, struggles.

6

A seductive dance
despair—devil's calling card
and dark choreography.

7

How do you confess
sins against a priest to him?
I haven't the courage.

8

Caught in liar's teeth
absolution springs the snare—
no longer victim.

9

Gideon's ephod — an
idol to appetites
reigns in my kitchen.

10

Like hairs on our heads,
many are the thoughts of our hearts —
some need cutting off!

11

Trouble follows me
nipping at my heels — it's bite
can't sink a heart at peace.

12

A river of thoughts
raft around stones of doctrine —
risk roving adrift.

13

Sad hearts drag their house,
and all they own—so wealthy,
can't squeeze through the gate.

14

Do plans, lists matter?
Only when my distant view
is like the rich man's.

15

A good hard scrubbing
removes the dark rust of sins,
restores God's bright love.

16

Living flawed stories,
plots, plans made into idols—
only God can save.

17

Wounds sealed, glossed over
fester under the surface—
will break open . . .when?

18

The light of Christ burns
for those seeking forgiveness—
I sit in the dark.

19

Twelve stones in Jordan's
riverbed keep two thousand
years of sins washed clean.

20

Contrite tears mingle
with absolving waters—
sins tumble downstream.

21

Place all in God's hands—
reconciliation teaches
that we will not die.

22

My pierced pride pricked, drained,
lays hollow while waiting
Holy Spirit's breath.

23

Bitter judgmental
words heaved through the hushed chapel
clattered to the floor.

24

Fans, friction, fragments—
wounded, broken to be shared,
pride prevents yielding.

25

Lacking confession
my sins slip unresolved—
lurch unabsolved.

26

What parts need to die—
to be left in Lazarus' tomb—
keep me from new life?

27

Collapsing under
my own weight like pent beached whales—
needing a Savior.

28

Grave danger illusion,
wanting to be God ourselves—
remember He died upon a cross.

29

Evil prowls now, here—
stomping on truth, beauty—
the cross vanquishes.

30

Darkness holds its breath,
straining to see the dayspring
born from on high.

31

Bright pinpoint of light—
a star held in vast darkness,
our soul rests alone.

32

Bring light to the world,
not a refractory heat—
illume with vivid truth.

33

God, taking flesh, bone—
human-ness from Mary's womb
united in one.

34

Born of a woman
keeping all things in her heart,
as He's in our hearts.

35

Leap from the manger
to the mystery of God—
Father, Son, Spirit.

36

Not just one day— or
a season, incarnation
abides eternal.

37

The real King's story
of Advent expectation—
God's love defeats death.

38

Alone before God,
my tears pounding with clenched heart—
soul's aphonic scream.

39

Wiping clumps of hair
kneeling on the bathroom floor—
we both cry, why Lord?

40

Death buries the *why? why?*
shrouded with linen and myrrh
deep in silent tomb.

41

Grieving tears well up
flinching wounds, loss, shame confessed—
forgiven? absolved?

42

Brooding injury—
Marionite's love, wisdom
soothes a broken heart.

43

Suffering softens
stones—malleable, now shaped like
new believing hearts.

44

World plights, politics,
brutal ideologies,
kitchen table talks.

45

My heavy burdens
are but feathers in God's hand—
light He carries me.

46

My soul is restless,
no peace under golden skies—
ten angels pray for me.

47

Take my wounded heart
thrown at God's feet to step on . . .
grace treads so lightly.

48

If, like mourning doves
I spurn earth and soar towards You,
then my heart rejoices.

49

Set aside duty,
resentment—pick up the prose
of a pierced heart.

50

Immersed in Jesus,
this human mind, drowning heart
gasp—breathe mystery.

51

God stoop down, touch me—
I crave your healing caress,
a balm for my soul.

52

Breath of God come, burst
into life—inflame hearts
and burn away fear.

53

Do not grow weary,
your heavy stony heart seeks
those two, three who pray.

54

Lord, how I attend
my garden of grudges—weed,
water resentments.

Until they grow strong
roots in the soil of my heart,
fearful of pruning.

55

Lord, let me become
the trod-upon worn doorstep
to the King's highway.

56

Loving self badly,
I lost self. Seeking just You,
I found both of us.

57

God wastes not one thing,
each scrap of experience
nailed—builds up the cross.

58

Love's heat burns away
debris, underbrush of sin,
yields fruitful ashes.

59

Follow me to the cross,
suffer and die—now
who do you say that you are?

60

God calls me Trust, but
Worry is my other name—
anxious pseudonym.

61

The cross plunges deep
into the hearts of God's chosen—
His prepared soil.

62

Bone against raw bone
rubbing my weary spirit—
the weight of the cross.

63

Even though called tender,
money cannot offer comfort
like tenderness of God.

64

Words breaking open,
letters show forth their wisdom—
God's unchanging voice.

65

Relieved that God writes
straight with my crooked lifelines,
zig-zag decisions.

66

Good and holy mask
removed, reveals selfish airs—
receive a new face.

67

Can I accept change?
Only through God's gift—graceful
lilies of spring days.

68

A bleeding world weeps,
torrents of trials, dreams doused—
love staunches the flow.

69

I am not the pot
broken, mended with faint glue—
I am the piercing light!

70

Authority's voice
calms seas of concern, quells
unclean spirits.

71

Reach upward to Him
for He makes us His children
sharers in divine.

72

God drops a ladder
thronged with angels in my yard—
will I climb to glory?

73

God drops a ladder
thronged with angels in my yard—
the Lord is in this place!

74

Painted blood drips
wounded washes of color—
God's canvas of grace.

75

He sighs, *Ephphatha!*
God has sent us a trumpet—
open your ears, hear!

76

Such deep muck and mud
He has to wade and push through
to dwell in me.

77

Stumbling darkness
staggers away when hearts ignite—
conversion stories.

78

My cross will never
break your back, bend you double,
too heavy to lift.

79

My net is empty—
accept His invitation
go into the deep.

80

Walk out of that boat,
drop overboard squalling fear—
He says to you, *Come.*

81

Talk of love is cheap—
keeping the laws, commandments
sacrificial work.

82

Doubts, lay 'em all down,
then take up the yoke of faith—
the Lord's light burden.

83

Don't cling to hardness
which sinks like a rock—float in
a river of grace.

84

Martha, sleeves rolled up,
dishrag in hand, vain cleaning—
otiose serving.

85

A mature spirit—
willing to yield to unseen,
to be dependent.

86

Young Daniel's wisdom
sets all free from injustice,
just like Susanna.

87

Choose her: discipline.
Bow down, accept her fetters—
thus, she becomes joy.

88

You know I love you,
Lord — Peter's protest and mine.
He says, *follow me.*

89

Saint Peter's fish tale —
cast your net on the right side,
catch all the nations.

90

Life is not to grab,
but surrender — become
entirely new gift.

91

Golden words, wise pearls,
treasure held in clay vessels
made to be broken.

92

I don't get those poems
that extol the ordinary
and don't acclaim God.

93

Thoughtful art crafted
to evoke a vision, truth—
authentic longing.

94

Little San Juan, your
runny nose blends the charcoal
mustache, drawn with care.

95

A just Everyman,
faith-filled, with a longing heart—
Job wants to see God.

96

Hands of Sophia
weave a knowing tapestry,
threads of divine love.

97

Paschal mystery—
red beeping lights, oxygen hiss—
rising to new life!

98

Flying higher—against
asphyxiating limits
of being earthbound.

99

Dressed in blue, standing
at the foot of her deathbed,
His light fills the room.

100

Humbled, on my knees,
obedient to the cross +
raised in this breaking.

101

His divine breath, Word
also brought forth sky, earth, sea —
brings dead back to life.

102

My gaze follows Mary's
over the still pond beyond —
quiet sign of hope.

103

We gather, filling
the pews with our lives — broken,
burdened, offering all.

104

The vine shoots around
the chapel walls broadcasting
significant symbols.

105

Mary—undo knots
of discord tied by children
too spiteful and proud.

106

Faithful lives braided
into one praising story—
strands twenty years long.

107

Suffering much—blind,
lame, deaf and poor, come worship—
anointed with oil.

108

Newly anointed
with Chrism—her face, hair shine,
dressed in gleamy white.

109

A time for endings—
new beginnings, smallest steps
toddling toward God.

110

Place your hand in mine
trusting like a little child—
I will lead you home.

111

In quiet worship
there is One Word of light,
reverent peace of prayer.

112

Invisible threads
weaves the maker of all things—
one holy fabric.

113

Cast-iron doctrine
when not tempered by mercy,
rusts, corrupts through zeal.

114

Saving bread, pure wine,
words broken and rent hearts shared—
kitchen table talks.

115

Preoccupations—
gossip, slander means scandal
to the Eucharist.

116

Altar stripped, exposed
to jeers—contempt of unbelief.
Insult breaks His heart.

117

Lord of history—
mystery hidden in bread—
future majesty.

118

Eat disgrace and shame,
get drunk on humbled scourged wine—
a glutton for Christ.

119

He came to give me
His holy divinity,
becoming flesh, blood.

120

Civilized chalice
stem gripped chest high, take and drink—
universe life's blood.

121

That round piece of bread
contains all the universe—
The Body of Christ.

122

Fear keeps us hiding,
locked behind indolent doors—
no flame ignited.

123

Holy Spirit blows
her wisdom like a storm through
rafters of my heart.

124

Their tongues were speaking
words on fire—some understood,
while others scoffed.

125

Sevenfold gifts descend,
riding upon heaven's wind—
howling through locked doors.

126

Red gladiolas
sing, *Come, come Holy Spirit!*
Their stamens are fire.

127

My constant companion,
a vibrant red restless flight—
wings beating toward love.

128

Her raiment of stars
herald a queen's stature
standing on the black moon.

129

If we lift the veil
oh, but if . . . if we just could —
what would God reveal?

130

Serene lamb's ears peep
over the weathered tombstone —
peace, life without end.

131

We are the stuff of stars —
glittering pieces of light,
all held in God's hand.